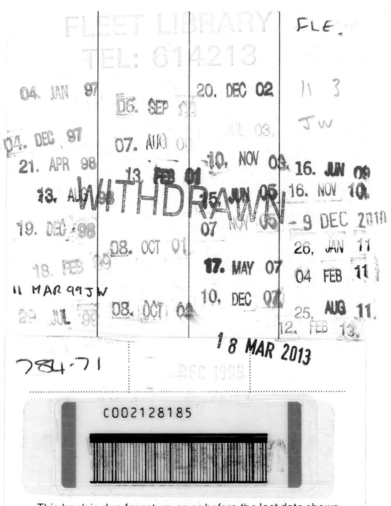

'BLESS 'EM ALL!'

'BLESS 'EM ALL!'

THE WORLD WAR TWO SONGBOOK

Denis Gifford

Foreword by Spike Milligan

Webb & Bower

MICHAEL JOSEPH

Other books by Denis Gifford

The Space Patrol Handbook
Cinema Britanico
British Cinema
Movie Monsters
Science Fiction Film
Discovering Comics
Stap Me! The British Newspaper Strip
Test Your NQ (Nostalgia Quotient)
50 Years of Radio Comedy
A Pictorial History of Horror Movies
The British Film Catalogue
Karloff: The Man, The Monster, The Movies
Chaplin
The Armchair Odeon
Victorian Comics
Happy Days: 100 Years of Comics
The British Comic Catalogue
The Great Cartoon Stars
Run Adolf Run

Monsters of the Movies
The Morecambe and Wise Comic Book
Stewpot's Fun Book
Quick On The Draw
The Two Ronnies Comic Book
Eric and Ernie's TV Fun Book
The Illustrated Who's Who in British Films
British Comics and Story Paper Price Guide
The International Book of Comics
The Golden Age of Radio
The Complete Catalogue of British Comics
British Animated Films
The Encyclopedia of Comic Characters
Eagle Book of Cutaways
Comics at War
The Comic Art of Charlie Chaplin
The Story Paper Price Guide
The Best of Eagle Annual

First published in Great Britain 1989 by
Webb & Bower (Publishers) Limited
5 Cathedral Close, Exeter, Devon EX1 1EZ
in association with Michael Joseph Limited
27 Wright's Lane, London W8 5TZ

Published in association with the Penguin Group
Penguin Books Ltd, Registered Offices: Harmondsworth
Middlesex, England
Viking Penguin Inc, 40 West 23rd Street, New York, New York 10010, USA
Penguin Books Australia Ltd, Ringwood, Victoria, Australia
Penguin Books Canada Ltd, 2801 John Street, Markham, Ontario
Canada L3R 1D4
Penguin Books (NZ) Ltd, 182–190 Wairau Road, Auckland 10, New Zealand

Designed by Vic Giolitto

Production by Nick Facer/Rob Kendrew

Introduction Copyright © 1989 Denis Gifford

Foreword Copyright © 1989 Spike Milligan Productions Limited

British Library Cataloguing in Publication Data

Gifford, Denis, *1927–*
    Bless 'em all! : the World War Two songbook
    1. Popular songs in English, 1939–1945 –
    Collections
    I. Title
    784'.0942

ISBN 0-86350-355-1

Typeset in Great Britain by P&M Typesetting Ltd, Exeter.

Colour reproduction by Peninsular Repro Service Ltd, Exeter, Devon.

Mono reproduction by Butler & Tanner Ltd, Frome and London

Printed and bound in Great Britain by Butler & Tanner Ltd, Frome and London

CONTENTS

FOREWORD

Writing the foreword to this Second World War songbook is very nostalgic, for as a young soldier I formed a dance-band and we played every tune that is listed in this book. We learned the songs by listening to an old Cassor radio in the NAAFI; in those dark days, music played a major role in everyday soldiers' lives. When we played at dances soldiers would come to the stand and ask for requests. Of course they were usually love songs: 'Please can you play *That Lovely Weekend*'. That was one of the most requested, along with *He Wears a Pair of Silver Wings* and *These Foolish Things* – it meant a lot to them.

Sometimes all the dancers would sing the words, especially the last waltz *Who's Taking You Home Tonight?* It was a very moving experience. It was a song of hope for the many young servicemen who did not know if they would live to see the end of the war. Of course there were the drunks – 'I shay can you pleach play *Bang Away Lulu*', it was all part and parcel of those stirring times. I once met Churchill's chauffeur, a Corporal Weeks, who told me that the great man would often sing to himself in the back of the car – a particular favourite of his was *Hang Out the Washing on the Siegfried Line*.

During those unforgettable years dance-bands throughout Britain were playing the songs from this book: from NAAFI pianists to Carroll Gibbons and his band at the Savoy. Ironically Ken 'Snakehips' Johnson and his band at the Café de Paris were playing *When They Sound the Last All-Clear*, when a bomb dropped, killing most of the band.

I remember when in an Observation Post in Italy in the middle of the battle for Cassino, I was trying to find our battery network on my wireless when I stumbled across the Allied Forces network and heard Anne Shelton singing *White Cliffs of Dover* and I burst into tears. There were amusing times as well. Advancing up Italy, we camped next to a damaged church. The pianist, one Harry Edgington, found the organ – it was quite something to hear him telling the priest how to sing *Oh! What a Surprise for the Du-ce*, (it was a bigger surprise for the priest when he found out what he was singing). .

One of the most moving occasions was on a dark, rainy night in North Africa, hearing German soldiers sing *Lilli Marlene* as they were marched to a prisoner-of-war camp. Indeed, the music of the Second World War was universal: GIs sang *Ma I Miss Your Apple Pie*; Italians sang *Oi Marie*; French *poilus* sang *Alouette*. In those times music was as important as ammunition. When HMS *Kelly* sank off Crete, as the survivors clung to life-rafts, Captain Louis Mountbatten made them sing *Roll Out the Barrel*. Napoleon said 'An Army marches on its stomach', he should have added, 'they also march on their songs.' This book is a little time capsule from those distant days.

Spike Milligan

INTRODUCTION

'A JOLLY GOOD SONG WILL HELP TO WIN THE WAR!'

Says Colonel Algy Cholmondeley-Featherstonehaugh

Thumbing through my cupboardful of song copies, winnowing out the hundreds to make a concentrated choice to sum up six years of the songs that saw us through, I kept a spotter's eye open for one that would, in turn, sum up that summing-up and make a suitable title for this book. I found it in an old services song from prewar days, one that had been dusted down, polished up and blancoed for Civvy Street consumption by a clever pair of Tin Pan Alley tunesmiths, Jimmy Hughes and Frank Lake. As an ex-evacuee still knee-tanned under my unaccustomed long trousers, I knew nothing of the rudery of the original, as sung by those weary time-expired men on their 'heavily laden troopships just leaving Bombay bound for Old Blighty's Shore'. Nor, I suspect, did many of those who joined George Formby in the rousing chorus, in theatres, cinemas, or Anderson Shelters via the wireless or ten-inch Regal-Zonophone.

'Bless 'Em All' we sang, and meant it: the Long and the Short and the Tall, the Sergeants and WOIs, the Corporals and their Blinkin' Sons. And it doesn't matter, now that we know, that the Boys, as Vera Lynn (and all of us) called them, sang a different verb than bless. It illustrates perfectly that double level of human behaviour that makes us British British: we will do the job or die, but we reserve the right to grouse while we are doing or dying.

So not only do we who stayed at home during those terrible years, who were 'either too young or too old' (as Bette Davis lamented in *Hollywood Canteen*), bless all those who fought and worked for victory, we bless through this necessarily scanty souvenir those who gave us the songs to sing, and those who sang them to us.

When the war began on that September Sunday in 1939, there was already more than one song on the stocks suited to the occasion. Just as a far-sighted government had given us gas masks and were ready with sandbags and ration books, so the songwriters of Denmark Street were ready with words and music tuned to make us cheerful, tearful, patriotic or propagandic.

But first, before the new ones could be rushed to printer or plugger, there were two titles which, by chance or crystal ball were made for the moment. Gracie Fields, 'Our Gracie' to the entire British Empire, had her new film, *Shipyard Sally*, on September release. In it she sang the most perfect song for the Boys to sing as they marched away to war: *Wish Me Luck As You Wave Me Goodbye*. At the same time, a minor film company called Vogue Productions had just finished a film called *Discoveries*, based on Carroll Levis's popular radio show. With unusual showbiz flair they hurriedly shot a brand new finale, tacking it on to the end in time

for the trade show: Master Glyn Davies, a Welsh boy soprano snappily suited in a Naval middy uniform, and supported by as many marching extras as could be bell-bottomed by the wardrobe department, sang *There'll Always Be An England*. This patriotic piece penned by Ross Parker and Hughie Charles, was the first soul-stirrer of a war which would not be noted for its stirring of souls. Ross and Hughie, however, soon caught the mood of the times and before the autumn ended came up with *We'll Meet Again* ('Don't Know Where, Don't Know When – But I Know We'll Meet Again Some Sunny Day'), a sentimental heart-wrencher with an optimistic uplift that would be the first wartime hit for Vera Lynn, soon to be nominated 'The Sweetheart of the Forces'.

There were other songs already out which would be snapped up and sung by the Boys as they marched away, or the Girls they left behind; making Thingummybobs that Help to Win the War to the sound of *Music While You Work* over the loudspeakers. There was *The Beer Barrel Polka* colloquially known by its chorus, 'Roll out the barrel', belted out so frequently by Bertha Willmott that it

virtually became her signature tune. There was *South of the Border*, which had surprised its British composers, Jimmy Kennedy and Michael Carr, when Hollywood cowboy Gene Autry lassoed it for one of his films. Now they were surprised again when soldiers took to singing it on their marches. Out it came again, publisher Peter Maurice taking the Mexican Senorita off the cover and replacing her with a squad of Scotties in the rain, subtitling it 'The Tommie's Theme Song'. Another song already being sung was *Run Rabbit Run*, a Noel Gay contribution to *The Little Dog Laughed*, George Black's London Palladium show. A news item about a couple of bunnies being shot up in the Shetlands by the Luftwaffe zoomed the song into renewed popularity. The show's stars, the beloved double act of Bud Flanagan and Chesney Allen, learned a new version, *Run Adolf Run!*

The anti-Hitler songs were hilarious – at the time, of course – and such pieces as *Adolf* (written by Annette Mills in her pre-Muffin the Mule period) with its 'naughty boy' approach ('Come on, hold your hand out, we're all fed up with you, Cor Blimey!') *It's Just Too Bad for Nasty Uncle Adolf*, *Who Is That Man Who Looks Like Charlie Chaplin*, *Old Man Schicklegrubber*, and the Mussolini song, *Oh! What a Surprise for the Duce* ('They do say, he's had no spaghetti for weeks!'), still managed to stay this side of the uproarious rudery of the Walt Disney version, once the Yanks came. in: 'Ve heil (*razz!*) heil (*razz!*), right in *Der Fuhrer's Face!*'

The optimism of the Phoney War, the months that would lead to Dunkirk, was never better summed up than in the song, sung by that same Flanagan and Allen, *The Washing on the Siegfried Line*. It was written by Kennedy and Carr, who were inspired by a cartoon in the *Daily Express*. Bobbie St John Cooper, a brilliant staff artist, had created 'Young Bert', hoping to do for the Second World War what Bruce Bairnsfather had done for the First World War with his 'Old Bill'. Young Bert, somewhere in France (another phrase of the days used to good effect by the popular song writers), wrote home to Mum that he was sending her a length of Hitler's Siegfried Line to hang her washing on. Kennedy and Carr snapped it up right away, and although the ubiquitous Ross Parker and Hughie Charles co-opted Cooper with their 'official' musical version of the joke, *I'm Sending You the Siegfried Line to Hang Your Washing On* failed to make the hit parade.

The first great heart-breaker of the war was, without doubt,

Goodnight Children Everywhere, a song whose cover bore the phrase, 'With a tender thought to all evacuated children'. The title was taken from the famous closing line all listeners to the BBC *Children's Hour* knew by heart, spoken with a short pause between 'children' and 'everywhere' by Uncle Mac, as Derek McCulloch was universally known. Both children, far from home, and lonely mothers, many without husbands now, must have wept openly when Our Gracie, at her homeliest and tenderest, sang 'Your mother thinks of you tonight...' She followed through with another punch to the heart at Christmas: *I'm Sending a Letter to Santa Claus* ('To bring Daddy safely home to me').

Fortunately there was still plenty to laugh at, especially on the Home Front. Fruity Arthur Riscoe, having sung *Goodbye Sally*, told us to *Follow the White Line All the Way*, celebrating the Great White Line that now divided every road in England into two ('Starting at the Rose and Crown!'). The Two Leslies (Sarony and Holmes) sang *Good Night* ('Got your torchlight? Got your gas mask? All right!').

There were slogan songs: *Go To It!*, *Dig Dig Dig for Victory!* and *Up Housewives and At 'em!* There were songs about the Army (*Good Morning Sergeant-Major*); the Navy (*Sailor Who Are You Dreaming of Tonight*); the RAF (*I Fell in Love with an Airman who had Big Blue Eyes, but I'm Nobody's Sweetheart Now*); the Home Guard (*When the Lads of the Village Get Crackin'*); the blackout (*Everybody Do the Blackout Stroll*); rationing (*Somebody's Pinching My Butter*); long-lost luxuries (*Bring Me Back a Banana, Sailor Boy*); the GIs (*Got Any Gum, Chum?*); the Allies (*My Sister and I*: 'but we don't talk about that'); Winston Churchill (*We'll Follow the Man Who Smokes a Big Cigar*); lend-lease (*Thanks Mister Roosevelt*); refugees (*Thanks for Dropping In, Mister Hess*); the future (*It's a Lovely Day Tomorrow*) and victory ('High and low, great and small, they'll all be dancing at *The Victory Ball*').

Ironic, then, that perhaps the greatest song of the Second World War should be shared by both sides, the story of the German girl who waits underneath the lamplight, by the barrack gate: *Lilli Marlene*, proving for all time that love is greater than war.

Denis Gifford
Sydenham

The title of this Introduction is all I recall of a song I heard once on the wireless in 1939.

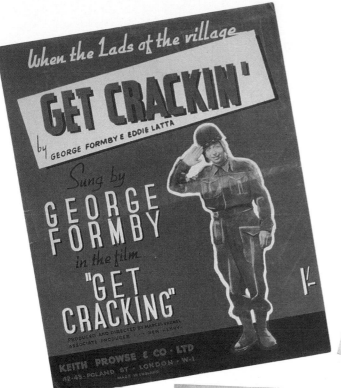

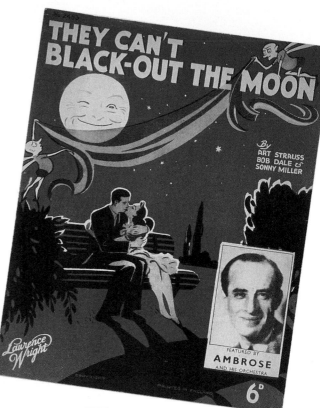

There'll always be an England

Sung by GLYN DAVIES in CARROLL LEVIS' FILM 'DISCOVERIES'

Words & Music by ROSS PARKER & HUGHIE CHARLES

A VOGUE PRODUCTION

Irwin Dash Music Co. Ltd.
17, BERNERS ST., LONDON, W.1
Put DASH in your Programmes

1/-

THERE'LL ALWAYS BE AN ENGLAND

ROSS PARKER &
HUGHIE CHARLES

PUT **DASH** IN YOUR PROGRAMMES

14

-side a field of grain. THERE'LL ALWAYS BE AN ENGLAND While there's a bu-sy street; Wher-ev-er there's a

turn-ing wheel A mil-lion march-ing feet. Red, white and blue, What does it mean to you? Sure-ly you're

proud, shout it a loud, Brit-ons a-wake, The Em-pire too, we can de-pend on you, Free-dom re-

-mains these are the chains, nothing can break. THERE'LL ALWAYS BE AN ENGLAND And England shall be free. If

Eng-land means as much to you As Eng-land means to me. THERE'LL England means to me

RUN. RABBIT, - RUN!

Words by
**NOEL GAY &
RALPH BUTLER**

Music by
NOEL GAY

From

The Little Dog Laughed

GEORGE BLACK'S SHOW SHOP of 1939

6D

NOEL GAY
MUSIC COMPANY LTD
33, SOHO SQUARE. W.1.

FEATURED, BROADCAST &
RECORDED BY
JACK HYLTON
AND HIS BAND

Sing a "GAY" Song – Play a "GAY" Tune

RUN, RABBIT,–RUN!

Words by
**NOEL GAY &
RALPH BUTLER**

VERSE *Not too fast*

Music by
NOEL GAY

★ SEE OVER FOR PARODY CHORUSES

PARODY CHORUSES ON
"RUN, RABBIT, - RUN!"

*

RUN, ADOLF, RUN ADOLF, RUN, RUN, RUN, —
    LOOK WHAT YOU'VE BEEN GONE AND DONE, DONE, DONE, —
WE WILL KNOCK THE STUFFING OUT OF YOU;
    FIELD MARSHAL GOERING AND GOEBBELS TOO.
YOU'LL LOSE YOUR PLACE IN THE SUN, SUN, SUN;
    SOON YOU POOR DOG YOU'LL GET NONE, NONE, NONE.
YOU WILL FLOP WITH HERR VON RIBBENTROP, —
    SO, RUN ADOLF, RUN ADOLF, RUN, RUN, RUN.

RUN ADOLF, RUN ADOLF, RUN, RUN, RUN, —
    NOW THAT THE FUN HAS BEGUN, GUN, GUN;
P'RAPS YOU'LL JUST ALLOW US TO EXPLAIN, —
    WHAT WE DID ONCE, — WE CAN DO AGAIN.
WE'RE MAKING SHELLS BY THE TON, TON, TON.
    WE'VE GOT THE MEN AND THE MON, MON, MON.
POOR OLD SOUL, — YOU'LL NEED A RABBIT-HOLE, —
    SO, RUN ADOLF, RUN ADOLF, RUN, RUN, RUN.

*

COPYRIGHT BY

NOEL GAY MUSIC COMPANY LTD.,
33, SOHO SQUARE, LONDON, W.I.

Featured and Broadcast by **GRACIE FIELDS** in France

GOODNIGHT CHILDREN EVERYWHERE

With a tender thought to all Evacuated Children

Written & Composed by

GABY ROGERS

AND

HARRY PHILLIPS

"Harwood" 39.

The G. Norris MUSIC PUBLISHING Co Lt?, I, Norris St., LONDON S.W.I

6D NET

GOODNIGHT CHILDREN EV'RYWHERE

FOX-TROT BALLAD
(With a tender thought to all Evacuated Children)

Words and Music by

GABY ROGERS &
HARRY PHILLIPS

Lyrics under the staves:

1. Slee-py lit-tle eyes in a sleep-y lit-tle head, Slee-py time is draw-ing near. in a lit-tle while you'll be tucked up in your bed, Here's a song for ba-by dear.

2. Soon the moon will rise, and ca-ress you with it's beams, While the shad-ows soft-ly creep. With a hap-py smile you'll be wrapp'd up in your dreams, Ba-by will be fast a-sleep.

CHORUS

Good-night child-ren ev'ry-where, Your mum-my thinks of you to-

J.N.P.Co.   Printed by THE "A.A." PRESS Ltd, London, E.11

ss.167

2

WE'LL MEET AGAIN

Words and Music by

Tune Uke A. D. F#. B.

ROSS PARKER &
HUGHIE CHARLES

Let's say good - bye with a smile dear, Just for a while dear,____ We must part,
Af - ter the rain comes the rain - bow, You'll see the rain go,____ Nev - er fear,

Don't let the part - ing up - set you,____ I'll not for - get you sweet - heart.
We two can wait for to mor - row,____ Good-bye to sor - row my dear.

REFRAIN

WE'LL MEET A - GAIN don't know where, Don't know when, But I know we'll meet a -

☆Chord symbols for Piano-Accordion, Guitar & Banjo

PUT **DASH** IN YOUR PROGRAMMES

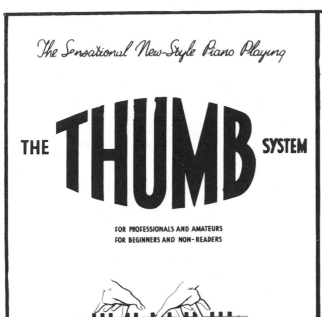

THEY CAN'T BLACK-OUT THE MOON

Written and Composed by

Tune Uke in C

G C E A
*ACCORDION

ART STRAUSS,
BOB DALE &
SONNY MILLER

Slowly

Key F

I'm not a - fraid of the dark, are you? are you? Gee but it's nice in the dark with the moon and you.

CHORUS

When we go strolling in the park at night, Oh! the dark-ness is a boon__ Who cares if we're with-out a light? THEY CAN'T BLACK-OUT THE MOON I see you smil-ing in the cig'rette glow, Tho' the

LAWRENCE WRIGHT MUSIC Co Ltd

Denmark St. London, W.C.2. Phone:- Temple Bar 2141/5.   Cables "Vocable London"   Telegrams "Vocable Westcent London" PRINTED IN ENGLAND

2546

Lawrence Wright's Sensational Successes

PLEASE LEAVE MY BUTTER ALONE

Written and Composed by

ANNETTE MILLS &
HORATIO NICHOLLS

GOOD LUCK, UNTIL WE MEET AGAIN

Written and Composed by

HORATIO NICHOLLS

KISS ME GOOD-NIGHT, SERGEANT-MAJOR

ART NOEL &
DON PELOSI

Pri-vate Jones came in one night Full of cheer and ve-ry bright

He'd been out all day up-on the spree _____ He bumped in-to Ser-geant Smeck

Put his arms a-round his neck And in his ear he whis-pered ten-der-ly. _____

*Symbols for Guitar, Banjo & Piano Accordion

1025

CHORUS

KISS ME GOOD-NIGHT SERGEANT-MAJOR_____ Tuck me in my lit-tle wood-en

bed _____ We all love you ser-geant-maj-or _____ When we hear you

bawl-ing "Show a leg"._____ Don't for-get to wake me in the morn — ing And

bring me round a nice hot cup of tea _____ KISS ME GOOD-NIGHT SERGEANT-MAJOR _____

_____ Ser-geant-Maj-or be a mo-ther to me. _____ me. _____

1025

Lowe & Brydone Printers, Ltd.
London. N W. 10
939

BRADBURY WOOD LTD.

PRESENT

TWO GREAT HITS

WISHING
(Will Make It So)

from the Film "LOVE AFFAIR"

Tune Uke
G C E A

Words and Music by

B. G. DE SYLVA

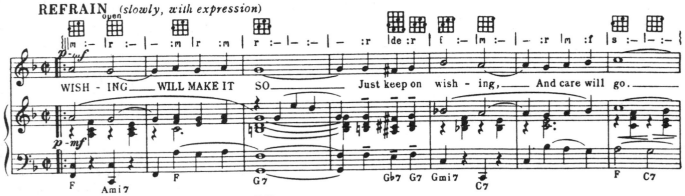

SING, MY HEART

from the Film "LOVE AFFAIR"

Words by
TED KOEHLER

Tune Uke
G C E A

Music by
HAROLD ARLEN

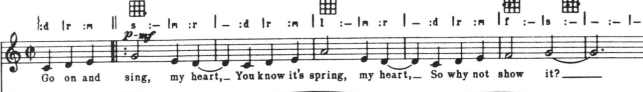

99ᴀ CHARING CROSS ROAD
LONDON. W.C. 2

ON SALE WHEREVER MUSIC IS SOLD

(We're Gonna Hang Out)

THE WASHING ON THE SIEGFRIED LINE

BY JIMMY KENNEDY & MICHAEL CARR

Featured with Enormous Success by
FLANAGAN & ALLEN

SIEGFRIED LINE

THE PETER MAURICE MUSIC CO. LTD

6 D. NET

(WE'RE GONNA HANG OUT)
THE WASHING ON THE SIEGFRIED LINE

Words and Music by

JIMMY KENNEDY &
MICHAEL CARR

Copyright MCMXXXIX for all Countries by

THE PETER MAURICE MUSIC Cº Ltd.

Maurice Building, Denmark St. London. W.C.2

Telephone: Temple Bar 3856 (5 lines)   Telegrams "Mauritunes Westcent London"

CHORUS

WE'RE GONNA HANG OUT THE WASH-ING ON THE SIEG-FRIED LINE Have you a-ny dir-ty wash-ing mo-ther

dear?___ WE'RE GON-NA HANG OUT THE WASH-ING ON THE SIEG-FRIED LINE 'Cos the wash-ing

day is here___ Wheth-er the weath-er may be wet or fine We'll just

rub a-long___ with-out a care___ WE'RE GON-NA HANG OUT THE WASHING ON THE SIEG-FRIED

LINE If the Sieg-fried Line's still there. WE'RE GON-NA there.___

We're gonna hang out the washing

The 2 Songs the Troops are Singing

SOUTH OF THE BORDER
(DOWN MEXICO WAY)

By JIMMY KENNEDY &
MICHAEL CARR

PRICE 6ᴰ PER COPY

THE HANDSOME TERRITORIAL

By JIMMY KENNEDY &
MICHAEL CARR

PRICE 6ᴰ PER COPY

THE PETER MAURICE MUSIC Cᴼ Lᵀᴰ
MAURICE BUILDING, DENMARK ST, LONDON. W.C.2.

No. 2481.
ADOLF
Words and Music by ANNETTE MILLS
6D.
Lawrence Wright
Copyright.
PRINTED IN ENGLAND

ADOLF

Tune Uke in C

G C E A
✳ ACCORDION

Written and Composed by

ANNETTE MILLS
Writer of
"BOOMPS-A-DAISY"

Tempo di marcia

1. A cer-tain Ger-man Chan-cel-lor has lost his head_____ He's go-ing to get a
2. We're sick of all the mud-dle and the mess you've made,_____ You've gone and stuck your

head-ache some-where else in -stead_____ and he will be re - tir-ing ve - ry
fin-gers in the mar - ma - lade,_____ So now you're go-ing to get a big sur-

soon_____ To join a cer-tain Kai- ser down at Doorn._____
-prise,_____ You're no-thing but a bas-ket-ful of lies._____

LAWRENCE WRIGHT MUSIC C⁰ Lᵗᵈ

Denmark St. London, W.C.2. Phone:- Temple Bar 2141/5 Cables:"Vocable London" Telegrams"Vocable Westcent London."

2543

PRINTED IN ENGLAND

CHORUS

A - DOLF__ you've bit-ten off__ much more than you can chew__

Come on hold your hand out__ we're all fed up with you (Cor blim-ey) A - DOLF

__ you tod-dle off__ and all your Na - zis too__ Or you may get

some-thing to re - mind You of the old Red White and Blue.__ Blue.__

Lawrence Wright's Sensational Successes

BOOMPS - A - DAISY

Written and Composed   by ANNETTE MILLS

GOOD LUCK, UNTIL WE MEET AGAIN

Written and Composed by   HORATIO NICHOLLS

OH! WHAT A SURPRISE FOR THE DU-CE!

(HE CAN'T PUT IT OVER THE GREEKS)

English Lyrics by
PHIL PARK

Music by
NINO CASIROLI

ΛOF

CHAPPELL
PRINTED IN ENGLAND

RECORDED AND BROADCAST
BY
FLORENCE DESMOND

1/- NET

1240

2"OH! WHAT A SURPRISE FOR THE DU-CE!"*
(HE CAN'T PUT IT OVER THE GREEKS)
*Pronounce Doo-chay

English Lyrics by
PHIL PARK

Tune Uke
G C E A

Music by
NINO CASIROLI

Valse brillante

PIANO

Doh = Eb

Poor Mus-so-li-ni Has got just a tee-ny Sus-pic-ion he's made a mis-take.

Say-ing the Med-i-ter-ra-ne-an Was an It-al-i-an lake.

Now must be reckoned As 'faux-pas' the sec-ond His Boast that in Greece he would win.

Now Ev-'ry day is a rain-y 'un What price that 'brist-ly chin!

See over for extra Verses and Choruses

4

EXTRA VERSES AND CHORUSES

2nd VERSE
When Count Ciano
Plays on the piano,
He can't see the stave or the clef.
There in the dark he is sheltering,
Dodging the rude R.A.F.
Dripping with medals
Ciano soft-pedals
'Cos Daddy in law's got the dumps
Half of his fleet's helter skeltering
Other half manning the pumps;

2nd CHORUS
Oh!— What a surprise for the Du-ce, the Du-ce,
He can't put it over the Greeks.
Oh!— What a surprise for the Du-ce, they do say
He's had such a kick in the breeks
Our navy likes its rum and rolls the barrel, the barrel,
The Du-ce's fleet is too discreet
I fear it's the sort that still sticks to its port.
Oh!— What a surprise for the Du-ce, the Du-ce,
He can't put it over the Greeks.

3rd VERSE
Il Tro-va-tor-e
Once caused a furor-e
But Musso has no time for this.
Too busy with his portfolio
Sorting out men to dismiss.
He's got a mania
There in Albania
Someone has certainly erred.
That is why Marshal Badoglio
Had to be given the bird:—

3rd CHORUS
Oh!— What a surprise for the Du-ce, the Du-ce,
He can't put it over the Greeks.
Oh!— What a surprise for the Du-ce, they do say
With Adolf his name simply reeks
Despondent are the famed Italian tenors— poor tenors
Sopranos sneeze on their top "E's"
Of Mezzos no trace, and a bomb on each 'base'
Oh!— What a surprise for the Du-ce, the Du-ce,
He can't put it over the Greeks.

Chappell

BLESS 'EM ALL

'THE SERVICE SONG'

KEITH PROWSE & Cº Lᵀᴰ
LONDON·W·1·

BY JIMMY HUGHES
AND FRANK LAKE

6ᴰ

MADE IN ENGLAND

BLESS 'EM ALL

Words & Music by
JIMMY HUGHES
& FRANK LAKE

* Soldier, Sailor (optional)

6119

"The Tutor without Rival"

THE
ECLIPSE
PIANOFORTE
TUTOR

By

Ernest Haywood

Clarity is the keynote of this new tutor, which is, indeed, a brilliant example of sound ideas, utilised to the best possible advantage in relation to present-day teaching methods. Lucid, yet containing a mine of useful information, perusal of its seventy pages will substantiate the claim that it is "The Tutor without rival."

ENGLISH FINGERING

CONTINENTAL FINGERING

2'6 NET

Obtainable from all Music Dealers

Publishers—

KEITH PROWSE & Co., Ltd., 42-43, Poland St.,
London, W.1

He wears a Pair of Silver Wings

as created by Miss Frances Day in:

BLACK VANITIES

George Black's

George Black's VANITIES

1/- NET

Lyric by Eric Maschwitz — Music by Michael Carr

A PAIR OF SILVER WINGS

Lyric by
ERIC MASCHWITZ

Tune Uke Bb. Eb. G. C.
*Accordeon

Music by
MICHAEL CARR

KEY Eb

It's just a sim-ple love af-fair, two peo-ple met, they learn'd to care,

And found them-selves in heav-en. To you may-be the stor-y's

noth-ing new, to me it's all my wild-est dreams come true.

Copyright MCMXLI for all Countries by

THE PETER MAURICE MUSIC Co. Ltd.

Maurice Building, Denmark St. London. W.C.2.

Telephone: Temple Bar 3856 (5 lines)   Telegrams: Mauritunes Westcent London

CHORUS

Al-tho' some peo-ple say he's just a cra-zy guy,— to me he means a mill-ion oth-er things— For

he's the one who taught this hap-py heart— of mine to fly, he wears A PAIR OF SIL-VER WINGS.

And tho' it's pret-ty tough the job he has to 'do,— I would-n't have him change it for a king's.— An

or-din-ar-y fel-low in a un-i-form of blue, he wears A PAIR OF SIL-VER WINGS.

A pair of silver wings

A pair of silver wings

THAT LOVELY WEEK-END

Words and Music by

MOIRA & TED HEATH

BRADBURY WOOD LTD
MUSIC PUBLISHERS
142 CHARING CROSS ROAD
LONDON, W.C.2

1/- NET.

7046

MADE IN ENGLAND

THAT LOVELY WEEK-END

Words and Music by

Tune Uke
Bb Eb G C

MOIRA & TED HEATH
Piano Score by FRANK FOX

Moderato *(with feeling)*

PIANO

Key = Eb

My darling, here's my letter, I'm writing through my tears, A few sweet words to thank you for lovely sou-ven-irs,

Mem-o-ries you gave me still ech-o in my heart, I'll dream of them while we're a - part.

REFRAIN

I haven't said thanks for that lovely week-end, Those two days of hea-ven you helped me to spend, The

thrill of your kiss as you stepped off the train, The smile in your eyes like the sun af-ter rain. To

1120

mark the oc-ca-sion we went out to dine, Re-member the laughter, the music the wine; That drive in the tax - i when

midnight had flown, Then breakfast next morning, just we two a - lone. You had to go, the time was so short, We

both had so much to say;— Your kit to be packed, the train to be caught, Sor-ry I cried but I

just felt that way. And now you have gone, dear, this letter I pen; My heart travels with you till we meet a - gain. Keep

smiling, my darling, and someday we'll spend A lifetime as sweet as that love-ly weekend. I love-ly weekend.

Lowe & Brydone Printers, Ltd.
London. N. W. 10

BRADBURY WOOD LTD.

PRESENT

TWO GREAT HITS

I Don't Want To Set The World On Fire

Words and Music by

EDDIE SEILER, SOL MARCUS
BENNIE BENJEMEN and
EDDIE DURHAM

REFRAIN

I don't want to set the world on fire,_____ I just want to start a flame in your heart._____

Copyright, MCMXLI, by Cherio Music Publishers Inc., New York

Price **1/-**net.

I Guess I'll Have To Dream The Rest

Words by
MICKEY STONER and
MARTIN BLOCK

Music by
HAROLD GREEN

REFRAIN

I guess I'll have to dream the rest   If you can't re-mem-ber the things that we said Those nights that my shoulder held

Copyright, MCMXLI, by Martin Block Publishing Cº

Price **1/-**net.

**142, CHARING CROSS ROAD
LONDON. W.C.2**

ON SALE WHEREVER MUSIC IS SOLD

Nº 413 A

MISTER BROWN
OF LONDON TOWN

FROM EMILE LITTLER'S SHOW - "MORE 1066."

WORDS & MUSIC BY
REGINALD ARKELL &
NOEL GAY

1/-

NOEL GAY MUSIC CO·LTD·33 SOHO SQ·LONDON W·1

MISTER BROWN OF LONDON TOWN

Words and Music by

Tune Uke G.C.E.A.

REGINALD ARKELL and
NOEL GAY

Bright,– Lambeth Walk Tempo

VERSE

Conversationally

KEY F

Mis-ter Brown of Lon-don Town Was hap-py as could be,–

Ev-'ry-thing was ap-ple-pie,– So far as he could see,– He'd got his wife,– he'd got his kids And

things were right as rain,– Un-til the God-for-sa-ken Hun Got bu-sy once a-gain. Then

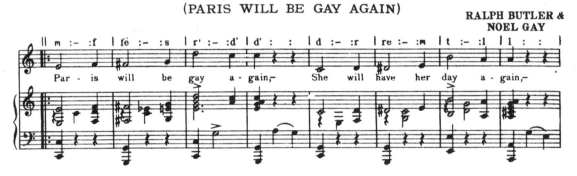

When they sound the last
'ALL CLEAR'

BY HUGH CHARLES   &   LOUIS ELTON

RECORDED & BROADCAST BY
VERA LYNN

1/-

Irwin Dash Music Co Ltd
17, BERNERS ST, LONDON, W.I
Put DASH in your Programmes

WHEN THEY SOUND THE LAST ALL CLEAR

Words and Music by

Tune Uke Bb. Eb. G. C.

HUGH CHARLES &
LOUIS ELTON

Key Bb

We've got our trou-bles and we've got our cares, But as

long as we keep smil-ing through,_____ There'll come a day when the

clouds roll a-way, And the sun will be shin-ing a-new.

PUT **DASH** IN YOUR PROGRAMMES

CHORUS

WHEN THEY SOUND THE LAST ALL CLEAR,_____ How hap-py my dar-ling we'll

be,_____ When they turn up the lights And the dark lone-ly nights, Are on-ly a

mem-o-ry,_____ Nev-er-more we'll be a-part,_____

Al-ways to-geth-er sweet-heart,_____ For the peace bells will ring And the whole world will

sing, WHEN THEY SOUND THE LAST ALL CLEAR. WHEN THEY CLEAR_____

I.D.S. 161

PUT **DASH** IN YOUR PROGRAMMES

[67]

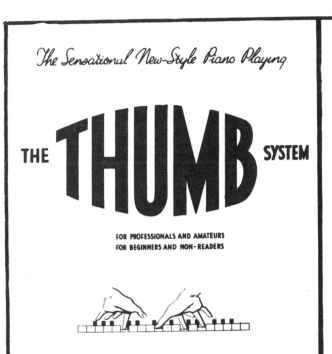
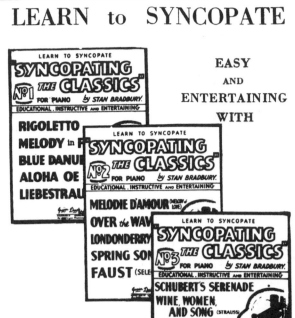

THERE'LL BE BLUE BIRDS OVER
THE WHITE CLIFFS OF DOVER

UKULELE GUITAR AND
PIANO ACCORDION ACC

PHOTO · WALTER BIRD

FEATURED AND
BROADCAST BY *Bebe Daniels*

Words by
NAT BURTON

Music by
WALTER KENT

1/- NETT

LONDON ENGLAND
B. FELDMAN & CO
125-9 SHAFTESBURY AV. W.C.2.
NEW YORK · SHAPIRO BERNSTEIN & CO INC

COPYRIGHT

There'll be Blue Birds over
The White Cliffs Of Dover

Additional Lyrics by D. ELVINS
Ukulele arranged by R. S. STODDON
(The Letters below Bass Stave indicate names of Chords for Guitar and Piano Accordion)

Words by
NAT BURTON

Music by
WALTER KENT

ROLAND'S PIANOFORTE T

(ENGLISH FINGERING)

PRICE 2

CHORUS *Slowly with expression*

There'll be Blue-birds ov-er THE WHITE CLIFFS OF DOVER, to-mor-row, just you wait and see.......... There'll be love and laughter and peace ev-er af-ter, to-mor-row, when the world is free.......... The shepherd will tend his sheep, The val-ley will bloom a-gain, And Jimmy will go to sleep In his own lit-tle room a-gain. There'll be Blue-birds ov-er THE WHITE CLIFFS OF DOVER, to-mor-row, just you wait and see.......... There'll be see..........

The white cliffs of Dover

THE BEST IN THE WORLD

T7d. EXTRA   [CONTINENTAL FINGERING]

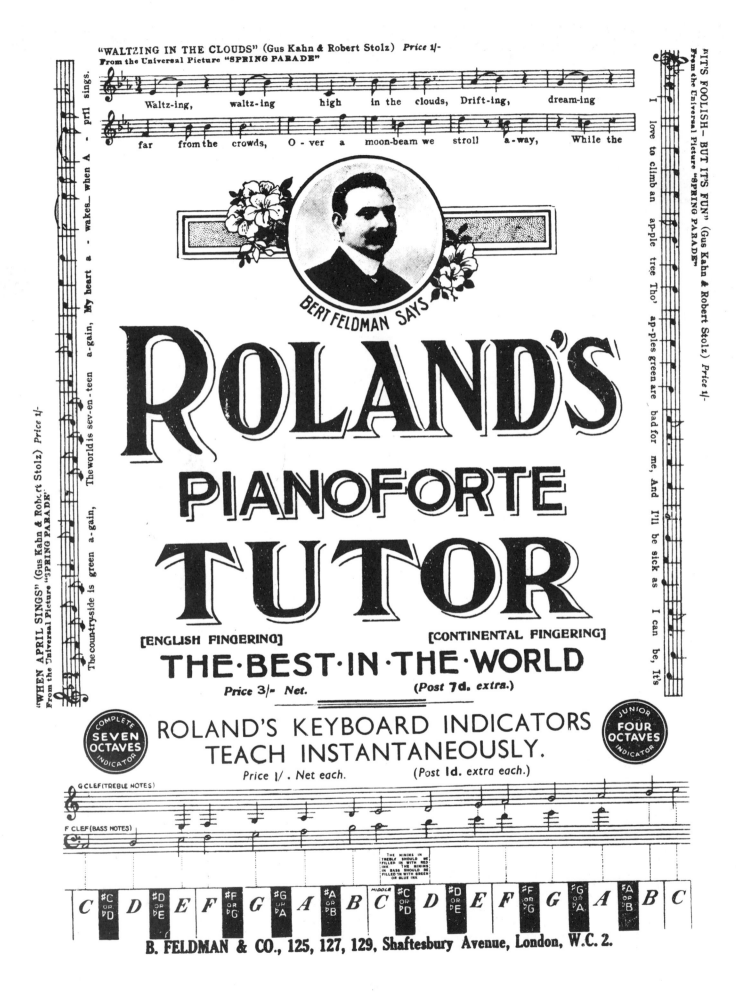

BERT FELDMAN SAYS

ROLAND'S
PIANOFORTE
TUTOR

[ENGLISH FINGERING] [CONTINENTAL FINGERING]

THE·BEST·IN·THE·WORLD

Price 3/- Net. (Post 7d. extra.)

COMPLETE SEVEN OCTAVES INDICATOR

JUNIOR FOUR OCTAVES INDICATOR

ROLAND'S KEYBOARD INDICATORS
TEACH INSTANTANEOUSLY.

Price 1/- Net each. (Post 1d. extra each.)

G CLEF (TREBLE NOTES)

F CLEF (BASS NOTES)

THE MINIMS IN TREBLE SHOULD BE FILLED IN WITH RED INK THE MINIMS IN BASS SHOULD BE FILLED IN WITH GREEN OR BLUE INK

C | #C or ♭D | D | #D or ♭E | E | F | #F or ♭G | G | #G or ♭A | A | #A or ♭B | B | C | #C or ♭D | D | #D or ♭E | E | F | #F or ♭G | G | #G or ♭A | A | #A or ♭B | B | C

MIDDLE C

B. FELDMAN & CO., 125, 127, 129, Shaftesbury Avenue, London, W.C. 2.

JOHNNY DOUGHBOY
FOUND A
ROSE IN IRELAND
Words and Music by
AL GOODHART
and
KAY TWOMEY
THE
STERLING
MUSIC PUBLISHING CO. LTD.
49-50 NEW BOND ST., LONDON, W.1.
CRAWFORD MUSIC CORP., N.Y.
AUTHORISED FOR SALE ONLY IN THE
BRITISH EMPIRE (Except Canada & Newfoundland)
MADE IN ENGLAND
166
1/-

Johnny Doughboy Found A Rose In Ireland

Words and Music by

Tune Uke
G C E A

AL GOODHART &
KAY TWOMEY

International Copyright Secured

1323

REFRAIN

Johnny Dough-boy found a rose in Ireland,_____ Sure the fair-est flow'r that Er-in ev-er grew._____ Oh, the blarney in her talk Took him back to old New York, Where his moth-er spoke the sweet-est blar-ney too_____ John-ny

842   Lowe & Brydone Printers, Ltd.
London. N.W.10

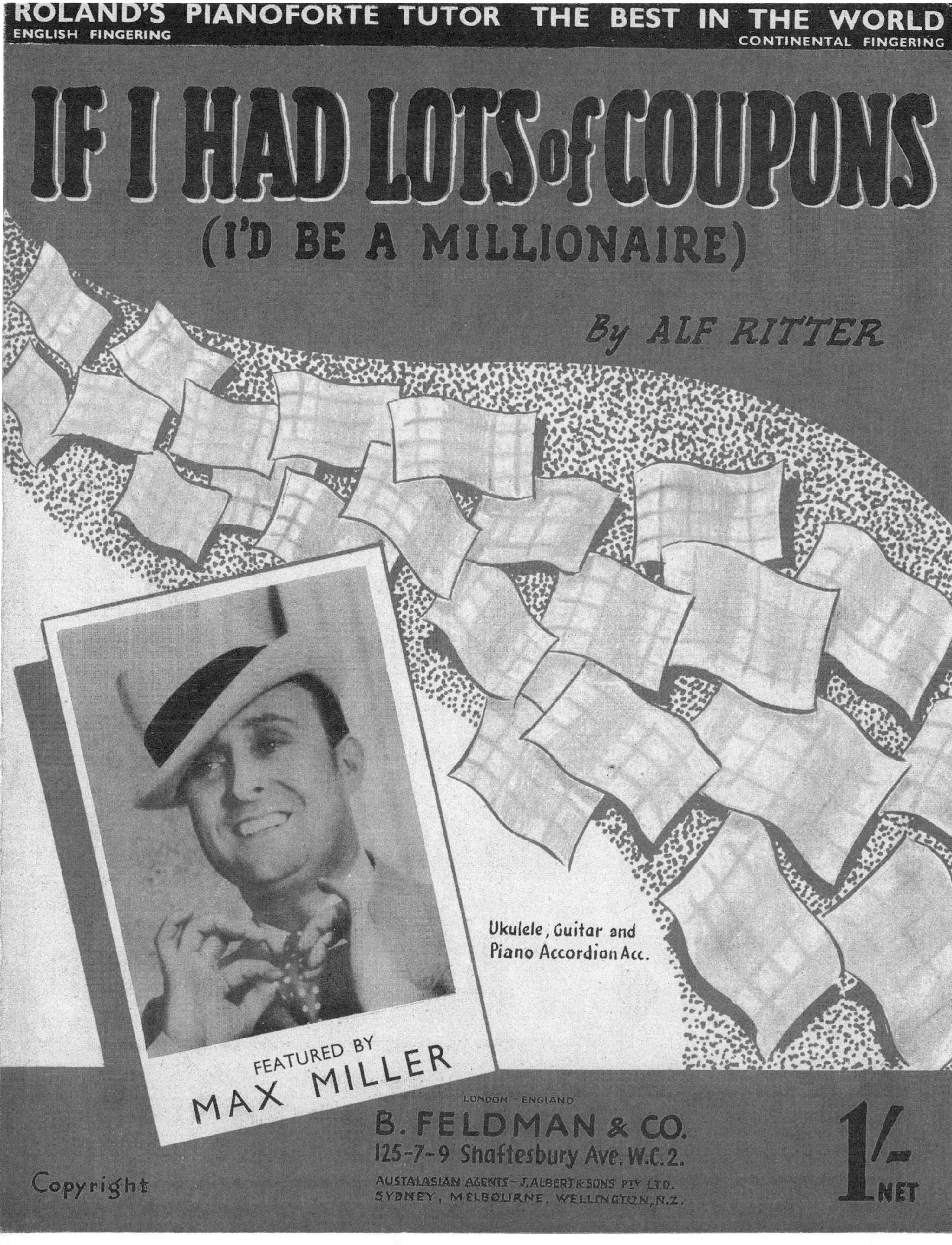
ROLAND'S PIANOFORTE TUTOR THE BEST IN THE WORLD
ENGLISH FINGERING
CONTINENTAL FINGERING
IF I HAD LOTS of COUPONS
(I'D BE A MILLIONAIRE)
By ALF RITTER
Ukulele, Guitar and
Piano Accordion Acc.
FEATURED BY
MAX MILLER
LONDON - ENGLAND
B. FELDMAN & CO.
125-7-9 Shaftesbury Ave. W.C.2.
AUSTRALASIAN AGENTS - J. ALBERT & SONS PTY LTD.
SYDNEY, MELBOURNE, WELLINGTON, N.Z.
Copyright
1/- NET

IF I HAD LOTS OF COUPONS
(I'D BE A MILLIONAIRE)

Ukulele arranged by R.S.STODDON

(The Letters below Bass Stave indicate names of Chords for Guitar and Piano Accordion)

ALF RITTER

Extra Verse
Now things have changed in many ways
I hate each little moth
'Cos they don't need no coupons
When they eat my table-cloth

ROLAND'S PIANOFORTE TUTOR.
(English Fingering)   *Price 3/- net*

com-fort, And would-n't have a care; Now I've got lots of mon-ey, But that don't mean a

thing, The things I want, well! I can't get, To rags I've got to cling. They are lit-tle bits of

pap-er, That you can't cash at the bank, And with-out those bits of pap-er, Then you've

got no chance to swank; *My socks are worn to tat-ters, *My stock-ings are in tat-ters, My shoes are worse for

wear, But if I had lots of cou-pons, Then I'd be a mil-lion-aire. If -aire.

If I had lots of coupons

*Female Version

THE BEST IN THE WORLD.

Post 7ᵈ extra.

(Continental Fingering)

[70]

When the Lads of the village

GET CRACKIN'

by GEORGE FORMBY & EDDIE LATTA

Sung by

GEORGE FORMBY

in the film

"GET CRACKING"

PRODUCED AND DIRECTED BY MARCEL VARNEL
ASSOCIATE PRODUCER ••• BEN HENRY•

1/-

KEITH PROWSE & CO • LTD
42·43·POLAND ST · LONDON · W·I
MADE IN ENGLAND

WHEN THE LADS OF THE VILLAGE
GET CRACKIN'

* Piano Accordion

Tune Uke: G C E A

Words and Music by
GEORGE FORMBY
& EDDIE LATTA

Hear those marching feet, down our Vil - lage street, It's the Home Guard
go - ing on par - ade._____ Ev' - ry Brit - ish son, should - er - ing a
gun, Out to show the stuff from which they're made _____ We're all

6320

4

Pub on the right ___ we stayed there all night, And the boys all smiled at
Poach-er, for fun ___ went bang with his gun At a rab-bit near a

me ___ I brought my py-jam-as, now don't say a word, I
tree ___ In div-ing for cov-er a rab-bit is fast, But

used to be a boy scout and so I came pre-pared, WHEN THE LADS OF THE VIL-LAGE GET
when we heard the gun go off the rab-bit was last, WHEN THE LADS OF THE VIL-LAGE GET

CRACK-IN' ___ Down the road to Vic-tor-y. WHEN THE
CRACK-IN' ___ Down the road to Vic-tor- -y.

LILLI MARLENE

Featured by
BILLY COTTON
AND HIS BAND

1/- NET

BY *NORBERT SCHULTZE*, *HANS LEIP* and *TOMMIE CONNOR*

LILLI MARLENE

(Pronounced "LILY MARLANE")

Words and Music by

Tune Uke G.C.E.A.
*Accordion

HANS LEIP
NORBERT SCHULTZE
& TOMMIE CONNOR

Un - der neath the lan-tern by the bar-rack gate, Dar-ling I re-member the way you used to wait;'Twas
Time would come for roll call, time for us to part, Dar-ling I'd caress you and press you to my heart; And

There that you whis-pered ten-der - ly, That you lov'd me, You'd al-ways be,
There 'neath that far off lan-tern light, I'd hold you tight, We'd kiss "Good-night;" My Lil - li of the

lamp - light, My own LIL-LI MAR - LENE.

Or-ders came for sail-ing some-where o-ver there, All con-fined to bar-racks was
Rest-ing in a bill-et just be-hind the line, Ev-en tho' we're part-ed your

more than I could bear; I knew you were wait-ing in the street, I heard your feet, But
lips are close to mine; You wait where that lan-tern soft-ly gleams, Your sweet face seems, To

could not meet; My Lil-li of the lamp-light, My own LIL-LI MAR-
haunt my dreams,

-LENE.

Lilli Marlene

3 Grand Songs!

PAPER DOLL

Words and Music by

JOHNNY S. BLACK

CHORUS
Slowly

I'm goin' to buy a PA-PER DOLL that I can call my own, A

SONS OF THE LORDS OF THE AIR

Words and Music by

DICK HURRAN

CHORUS

We're the SONS OF THE LORDS OF THE AIR _____ the A. T.

WHEN IT'S SUNSET IN THE HILLS
(OF OLD WYOMING)

Words by
TOMMIE CONNOR

Music by
HARRY RALTON

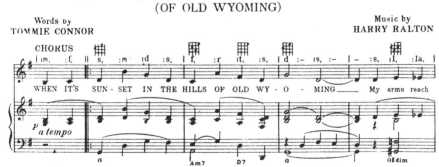

CHORUS

WHEN IT'S SUN-SET IN THE HILLS OF OLD WY-O-MING _____ My arms reach

Price 1/- Each

On sale at all Dealers or direct from ——

THE PETER MAURICE MUSIC Co., Ltd., Maurice Building, Denmark St., London, W.C.2.

I'M GOING TO GET LIT-UP

(WHEN THE LIGHTS GO UP IN LONDON)

WORDS & MUSIC BY HUBERT GREGG

FROM GEO. BLACK'S MUSICAL **STRIKE A NEW NOTE**

AT THE PRINCE OF WALES THEATRE

Featured & broadcast by **BILLY COTTON** AND HIS BAND

The PETER MAURICE MUSIC CO. LTD.

1/-

I'M GOING TO GET LIT-UP
(WHEN THE LIGHTS GO UP IN LONDON)

From Geo. Black's Musical "STRIKE A NEW NOTE" at The Prince of Wales Theatre

Words and Music by

HUBERT GREGG

Tune Uke G. C. E. A.
*Accordion

CHORUS *Brightly*

I'm going to get lit-up

more, much more, And be-fore the par-ty's played out, they will fetch the Fire Bri-gade out To the
canned, canned, canned, Thro' our Gins and An-go-stu-ras, we'll see lit-tle pale pink Fueh-rers, Hi de

F E7 Am E7 Am F Cdim C Cdim C A7 Ab A7

lit-test-up-pest scene you ev-er saw._____ I'm going to get saw._____
Heil-ing from the Cir-cus to the Strand._____ I'm going to get Strand._____

D7 G7 F G7 C C7 Cdim Fm6 C G7 C C7 Cdim Fm6 C

ADDITIONAL CHORUSES

3.

A regular flare-up when they light Trafalgar Square up,
A regular sight to open Nelson's other eye,
Through the day and through the night,
Signal beacons they will light,
"England this day expects the nation to be tight."
They'll have to stop traffic when they light Trafalgar Square up,
And down the rocky road to Westminster we'll reel, reel, reel,
What a shindy we will kick up,
Old Big Ben will chime a hiccup,
To epitomise the sentiments we feel.

4.

I'm going to get unsedately so serenely stinking
I'm going to get stinking as I've never been before,
When the dogs have had their day,
And the fight has had its fray,
We'll all be swapping battle-dress for bottle dress that day.
I'm going to get positively permanently pie-eyed,
The day we finally exterminate the Huns, Huns, Huns,
There'll be joy and there'll be laughter,
And there'll be no Morning After,
For we'll all be drunk for muns and muns and muns.

I'm going to get lit-up